KT-557-095

Cartoons and Animation

Richard Spilsbury

Heinemann
LIBRARY

www.heinemann.co.uk/library
Visit our website to find out more information about Heinemann Library books.

To order:
☎ Phone 44 (0) 1865 888066
📄 Send a fax to 44 (0) 1865 314091
💻 Visit the Heinemann Bookshop at www.heinemann.co.uk/library to browse
our catalogue and order online.

Produced for Heinemann Library by
White-Thomson Publishing Ltd,
Bridgewater Business Centre,
210 High Street, Lewes,
East Sussex BN7 2NH.

First published in Great Britain by Heinemann Library,
Jordan Hill, Oxford OX2 8EJ, part of Harcourt Education.
Heinemann Library is a registered trademark of
Harcourt Education Ltd.

© Harcourt Education Ltd 2007

Editorial: Clare Collinson, Melanie Waldron, Kate Buckingham
Consultant: Susie Hodge
Design: Tim Mayer
Picture Research: Amy Sparks
Production: Chroma Graphics

Originated by Modern Age Ltd
Printed and bound in China by South China Printing Company.

10 digit ISBN: 0 431 01473 6
13 digit ISBN: 978-0-431-01473-9

11 10 09 08 07
10 9 8 7 6 5 4 3 2 1

British Library Cataloguing in Publication Data
Spilsbury, Richard, 1963–
    Cartoons and animation. – (Art off the wall)
    741.5
A full catalogue record for this book is available from the British
Library.

Acknowledgements
The publishers would like to thank the following for their kind
permission to use their photographs:
akg-images pp. **5** (DreamWorks Pictures/Album), **10** (Album),
17 (Disney/Album), **18** (Walt Disney Productions/Album), **19** (Walt
Disney Productions/Album), **21** (DreamWorks Pictures/Album),
24–25 (Warner Bros./Album), **27** (Les Armasteurs/France 3 Cinema),
32 (Walt Disney Productions/Album), **34–35** (Disney/Album),
38 (Universal TV/20th Century Fox), **42** (Walt Disney
Productions/Album); Corbis pp. **7** (Hulton-Deutsch
Collection/Eadweard Muybridge), **11** (Patrick Pleul/epa), **14** (Louis
Quail), **15** (Louis Quail), **26–27** (DreamWorks SKG/Zuma),
29 (Warner Bros. Pictures/Bureau L.A. Collections), **31** (Louis
Quail), **36–37** (Bureau L.A. Collections), **39** (Courtesy of Warner
Bros./Bureau L.A. Collections), **44–45** (Tom Wagner), **47** (George
Hall), **50–51** (Jim Sugar); Getty Images pp. **13** (AFP), **45** (Stone),
46; The Kobal Collection pp. **9** (Mc Cay), **23** (20th Century
Fox/Barbara Nitke); Last Resort Picture Library pp. **48–49**; Science
Photo Library pp. **8** (Adam Hart-Davis), **33** (James King-Holmes);
TopFoto pp. **4**, **20**, **40–41** (Topham Picturepoint), **43**, **49**
(Esbin-anderson/The Image Works).

Cover photograph reproduced with permission of akg-images.

Every effort has been made to contact copyright
holders of any material reproduced in this book.
Any omissions will be rectified in subsequent
printings if notice is given to the publishers.

Contents

WOODMILL HIGH SCHOOL

Words appearing in the text in bold, **like this**, are explained in the Glossary.

Cartoons and animation

For many of us, the first memorable characters we saw on-screen were funny cartoon characters. Most of us have seen TV shows or films about birds that can talk, such as *Donald Duck*, or cats that can crumble to dust after an explosion and then miraculously recover, as in *Tom and Jerry*.

Cartoon characters often look like exaggerated versions of real creatures, but they may also be completely imaginary creatures, such as dragons or aliens. Cartoon characters can be anything from cars and trains to robots and pieces of furniture.

What is animation?

To animate means to bring to life. Animation is the process of photographing or filming a sequence of still images and showing them quickly one after the other to create the **illusion** of movement. The images used in cartoons are drawings or paintings.

But cartoons are just one type of animation. Other types of animation use three-dimensional (**3D**) models. These may be real models or **virtual** models created on computers.

The great thing about animation is that there is no limit to what you can put on-screen – almost anything can be made to appear to move, from broomsticks and lamps to dinosaurs and skeletons.

Like most real cats, Tom chases mice. Unlike real mice, Jerry usually comes out on top. Anything is possible in the world of cartoons.

Tricks of the trade

Throughout this book there will be examples of the skills and techniques animators use to convert their initial ideas into finished pieces. To create their invented worlds, animators have to come up with imaginative solutions, ranging from sound effects to **special effects**. When they are successful, we are drawn into the world their characters occupy.

The imaginary 3D world shown in the animated film *Madagascar*, was constructed entirely using computers.

Try it yourself

Throughout this book are suggestions for activities that you can try yourself. Most are simple exercises to do with particular stages in the animation process. These activities will help you build up skills which may be useful in making your own animated sequences or even films.

You can use the completed exercises as part of an animation **portfolio**. This is a collection of your best and most recent work, such as drawings, notes, and recorded animation clips. It is a record of your development as an animator.

moving pictures

People first discovered how to make still images appear to move in the 19th century. However, as a way of telling stories or passing on information, cartoons and animation have never been more popular and widespread than they are today.

Using your brain

What happens when we look at a picture? Eyes sense patterns of light and shade, as well as colour and shape. Nerves carry messages about what the eye has sensed to the brain. The brain then processes the information into an image. It compares it to other images we have seen before and allows us to recognize things.

Persistence of vision

When the brain processes information about an image, it retains the image for a brief moment of time before it is ready to process another image. The way the brain stores images in this way is called **persistence of vision**.

When a very slightly different image follows in quick succession, the brain blends together the stored image and the new image as if it is seeing a single image. Any minor differences between the two images are smoothed out.

When we see a series of slightly different images one after another, the brain merges the images together to give us the illusion of smooth motion.

The need for speed

The brain stores images for about one-twelfth of a second. When sequences of different pictures or individual **frames** are shown at 12 frames per second, or faster, they blend together creating the illusion of smooth movement. Any slower than this and the movement appears jerky.

Most cartoons and animated films are shown at 24 frames per second or faster to help make the movement appear smooth and realistic. That means each minute of film has over 1,400 separate frames. This is a major reason why cartoons and animated films take so long to make – they need a lot of drawings!

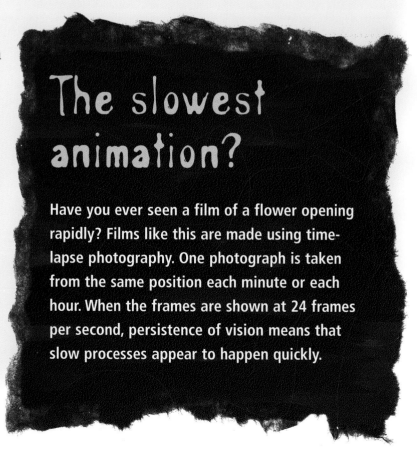

The slowest animation?

Have you ever seen a film of a flower opening rapidly? Films like this are made using time-lapse photography. One photograph is taken from the same position each minute or each hour. When the frames are shown at 24 frames per second, persistence of vision means that slow processes appear to happen quickly.

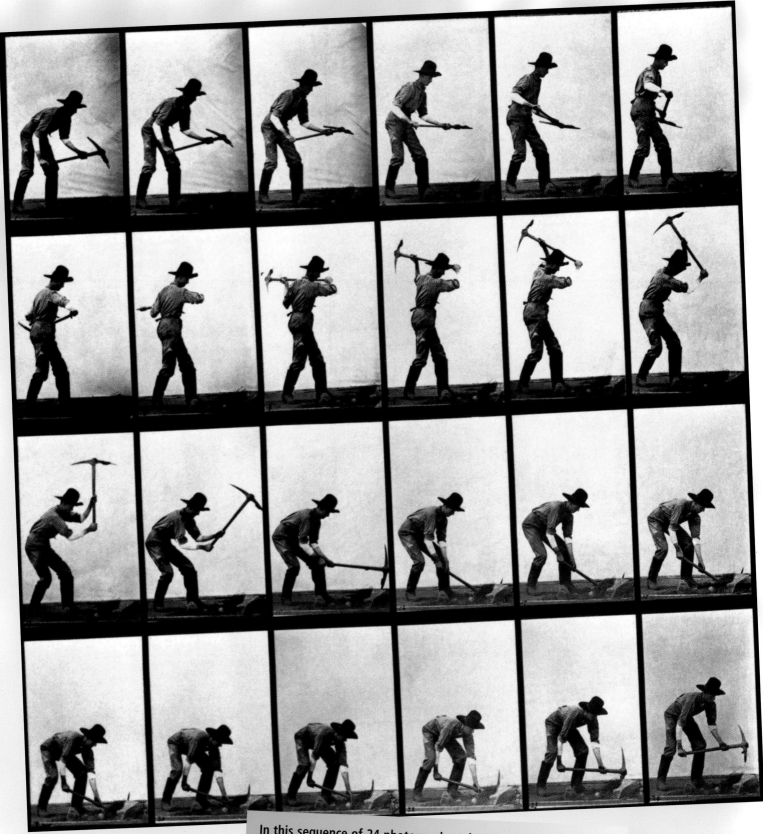

In this sequence of 24 photographs, taken in 1875, the position of the man changes slightly from one picture to the next. If the pictures were shown in quick succession, we would see the smooth movement of the man swinging his pickaxe.

How animation started

The first animated pictures were seen through magic lanterns and toys around the 1850s. Magic lanterns projected images on to a screen by shining light through glass slides that had photographs or painted pictures on them. A projectionist could create the illusion of movement by quickly changing the slides. People could also view short sequences of drawings using toys such as the **flickbook** and **zoetrope**.

Praxinoscopes

Animation took a great leap forward when Emile Reynaud invented the **praxinoscope** in 1877. Reynaud drew hundreds of drawings on to long strips of transparent film. He then wound the film by hand past a light and used mirrors to project the "moving" images on to a screen. This allowed much longer animations to be shown to audiences.

Cine cameras

Soon after Reynaud, the Lumière brothers developed cine cameras. These could be used to take sequences of photographs on long strips of film. With this new technology, cartoon makers could photograph different pictures, one at a time, on lengths of film. They could then run the sequences at speed to create animations.

The zoetrope is a horizontal drum with a strip of pictures inside and slots around the edge. By rotating the drum the pictures seen through the slots appear to move.

Winsor McCay drew and photographed each of the 10,000 pictures used to make the frames for his 1909 film *Gertie the Trained Dinosaur.*

Moving models

In the early 20th century, animators were already beginning to show weird and wonderful things on film using animation. The French film maker Georges Méliès loved magic shows and illusions. One day his cine camera jammed for a minute when he was filming in a street. When he was watching the film he noticed that, by chance, a bus had moved while the camera had been jammed and its place taken by a horse-drawn hearse. When he showed the film, the bus appeared to turn into a hearse. Méliès was the first film maker to use **stop motion** animation (see page 14).

Try it yourself

Your task is to create a short animation of someone jumping off a diving board. Stack 12 small pieces of paper together and staple them on the left-hand side. In pencil, draw on the top piece of paper a person standing on a diving board with a swimming pool below. The last picture will show a splash as they enter the water. The other pages should show the stages in-between. The person should change position only slightly from one picture to the next. When you flick the pages, the dive should be smooth. Top tip: make sure the diving board and the pool are always in the same position in each picture.

Animation studios

Early animators created their cartoons alone and their work was very time-consuming. But in the early 20th century there was a growing demand for **feature-length** animated films, and animators wanted to save time making them. So they formed animation studios and divided up the work between people with different skills and different roles. For example, artists created the drawings and cameramen photographed them.

In the 1930s, more and more studios were set up, including the Walt Disney Studio and Warner Brothers, and many animated films were made. Many of the original studios still survive alongside newer studios such as DreamWorks and Pixar.

Walt Disney is pictured here with his best-known cartoon character Mickey Mouse.

Creator focus: Walt Disney's studio

Walt Disney was the founder of the most famous cartoon animation studio of all. He moved the Walt Disney Studio from New York in 1923, where many animators worked, to Hollywood, California, the home of the US film industry. Here there were many technicians to produce his animated features. Walt Disney was a good artist but he only did the drawings for the studio's earliest films, such as *Steamboat Willy*, which was made in 1928. On later films, including *Snow White and the Seven Dwarfs* and *Pinocchio*, he employed artists such as Vladimir Tytla and Freddie Moore, who were able to make characters appear more realistic. The Disney look became popular across the United States and beyond. One of the studio's most famous cartoon characters, Mickey Mouse, remains the symbol of their global entertainment corporation.

This trainee pilot is practising landing in a flight simulator. He is landing on an animated representation of an airstrip.

The animated world

When televisions became more widespread in the 1950s and 1960s, people could see animation in their homes for the first time, not just at the cinema. At the beginning of the 21st century, animation can be seen on many different types of screen, from laptops and mobile phones, to enormous advertising hoardings on buildings and around sports grounds. Animation is no longer limited to short cartoons and feature films. It is used in interactive games on computers and consoles.

Beyond entertainment

Animation is also important in teaching complex subjects. For example, short animated sequences can help students visualize certain scientific processes such as reproduction or the formation of oil.

Flight simulators allow trainee pilots to learn how to operate complex and expensive aeroplanes before they use the real thing. Flight simulators have display screens showing animated versions of landing strips, created by computers, as well as different landscapes to fly over.

ways of animating

Traditionally, animation always involved photographing sequences of different drawings or models in different positions. But today most animation is created on-screen using powerful computers.

Time saver

Imagine having to copy or trace the drawings in each frame of a long cartoon. Thankfully, in 1915, J.R. Bray came up with the idea of **cels**. Cels are transparent sheets of film or **acetate**. Bray painted one background on paper and drew characters in different positions on separate cels that could be laid over the top of the background. This meant the background did not need to be redrawn for each frame. This saved animators a lot of time.

Building up pictures with cels

1. First a background is drawn or painted.
2. Outlines of characters are then sketched on paper in pencil.
3. A cel is placed over the background and a character is traced on to the cel in the right position, using the sketched outline.
4. The character is then painted in on the cel. For this it is necessary to use a permanent marker and/or paint mixed with a drop of washing-up liquid so the paint sticks to the surface of the cel.
5. Steps 3 and 4 are repeated for other characters, using separate cels for each character.
6. The background is then photographed, overlaid with all the cels together. This forms one frame.
7. To create the next frame, a new cel is created for each character that is to move. Only the bits that need new positions are redrawn. The parts that do not need to move are traced from the previous cel showing that character. Then the new cels and any cels that have not changed are laid over the background and another photograph is taken.

Are you registered?

When animators use cels, the sequences will appear jerky if the positions of characters and other objects relative to backgrounds shift about, even slightly. Animators avoid this by punching holes in the same place on each cel and placing them on metal pins so they are all in exactly the same position before they draw characters and other objects on the cels. This process is called **registration**.

This artist is tracing characters on to thin paper held in position by registration pins. He can use the sheets to create cels to overlay on backgrounds.

Try it yourself

If you have access to a digital camera, try using cels to make a cartoon dog walk. First create a background, such as a park. Then on an acetate sheet draw the dog starting its walk on the left-hand side. Create enough cels to show the different positions of the dog's legs as it walks to the right of the background. Photograph each cel against the background using the digital camera set up on a tripod or chair so it remains still and in the same place. When you run all the frames in sequence, your dog will appear to walk!

Stop motion animation

Have you ever seen the original *King Kong* film? Believe it or not, audiences in the 1930s were awestruck by the great gorilla climbing the Empire State Building. These sequences were created using stop motion animation. The basic process is to fix a model, such as Kong, in one pose, film or photograph it, stop the camera, change the pose a little, and then photograph the model again. When the individual frames are shown in quick succession, the model appears to be in motion.

Animators still use stop motion animation today. They often film models within detailed three-dimensional worlds, rather like mini stage sets, to make feature films such as *Chicken Run* and *The Corpse Bride*.

Trained beetles?

Around 1910, an animator called Ladislas Starevich made a stop motion film about a beetle called Leukanida and her two male suitors. He did it by filming dead beetles. However, his animation made the beetles appear to move so realistically that some journalists of the time claimed Starevich had filmed beetles that had been trained to act!

An animator repositions rabbits between frames for a sequence from Nick Park's stop motion film, *Wallace and Gromit: The Curse of the Were-Rabbit*.

As animators build up modelling clay around an armature, they check the proportions of the model are correct.

Try it yourself

Try making a model of a person using pipe cleaners and Plasticine. Twist together two pipe cleaners to make the backbone. At each end of the backbone, loop around a pipe cleaner to make the legs and arms. Leave a bit of the backbone sticking up above the arms for the neck. Cover the pipe cleaners with Plasticine, about 5 millimetres (0.2 inches) thick. Smooth the Plasticine over. Add a separate Plasticine head on to the neck and feet on to the legs. Remember to make the feet broad enough for the person to stand up. Take photographs of the model in different poses and from different angles and stick them on to a sheet of paper for your portfolio.

Model citizens

Some of the earliest stop motion animation used moveable toys such as teddy bears and dolls. However, to increase the range of facial expressions and movement, most animators create their own models. All kinds of models are created, from jointed wooden puppets to flexible clay figures. A soft, oily clay similar to Plasticine was used to make the models for Nick Park's *Wallace and Gromit* series of films (see page 30). Animators generally build up this clay around a jointed wire skeleton or **armature** to stiffen the models and allow particular poses to be held.

Escaping the cel

Today, cartoon creators mostly use computers to create animation. Some use a computerized version of traditional cel animation. Outline drawings of characters are scanned into computers or drawn directly on **graphics tablets** to produce outlines on-screen. The outlines can be coloured in and positioned against different backgrounds using graphics software. The final images are then converted into frames that are put together to form animated sequences.

Morphing

To cut down on the number of frames that need to be created, computers can be programmed to generate frames by themselves. This is called **morphing**. The start position and final position of a moving character are programmed into the computer. The computer then produces the frames for the character's positions in-between. Whether the character appears to move smoothly depends on how well the computer has been programmed to morph.

How do computers help animators?

Using graphics software to create animation means there is no need to trace any drawings to create new frames. This is because anything from the previous frames can be copied by the computer. Different elements within a frame can be changed without major redraws. For example, after watching an animation sequence an animator can change the colour of a character's clothes or smooth out a movement. Registration is also easier on a computer. Computers can accurately position characters against backgrounds.

Controlling movements

In computer animation, characters are given coordinates that determine their position on-screen, rather like map coordinates. To make a character appear to move, the animator changes its coordinates slightly from one frame to the next. This means that characters can be moved, rotated, stretched, enlarged, or reduced at the click of a few buttons, so there is no need for extensive redrawing.

A brief history of computer animation

Computer animation started in 1961 with the first computer game, *Spacewar*. This was created on an enormous computer by a researcher doing a university project. Animation development in the 1960s and 1970s was driven by aircraft manufacturing companies, which needed flight simulators to develop their products, and by games companies. However, computer animated effects began to appear in films, such as the Death Star diagram in *Star Wars*, made in 1977. The first completely computer animated feature film was *Toy Story* in 1995. Since then computer animation has progressed rapidly as the processing power of computers has increased.

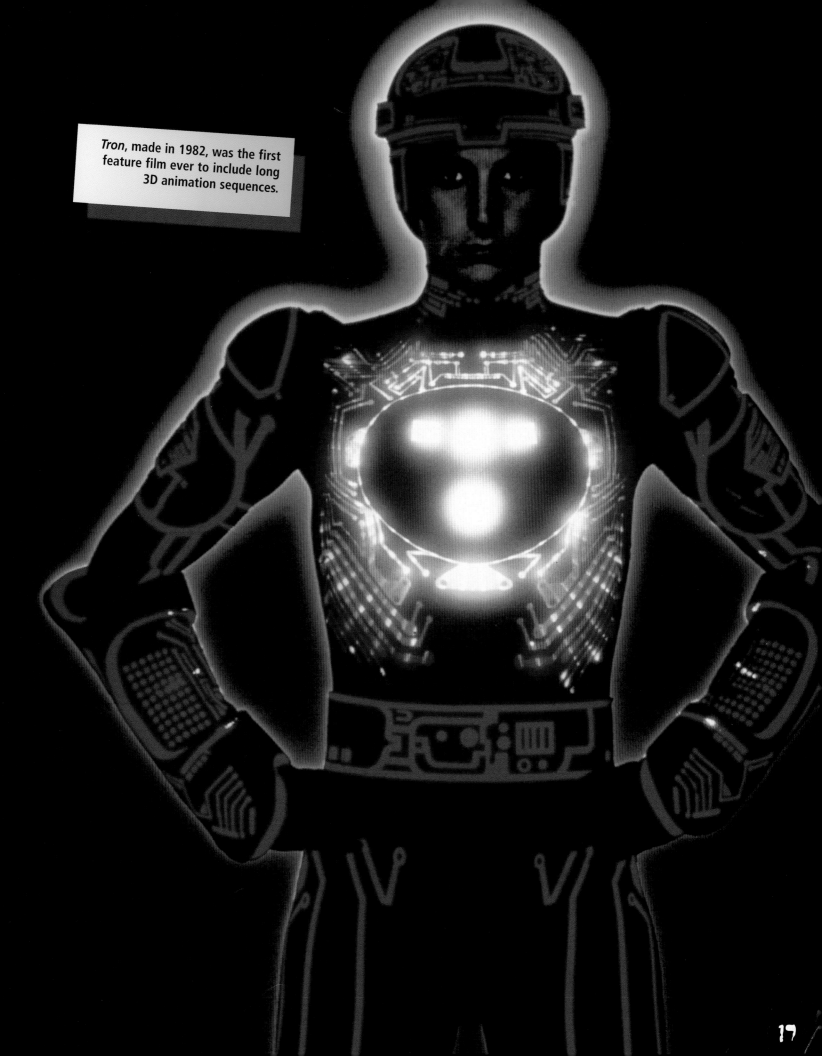

Tron, made in 1982, was the first feature film ever to include long 3D animation sequences.

A new dimension

In most TV cartoons, such as *Bugs Bunny* or *Futurama*, cel or on-screen animation is two dimensional (**2D**). Flat characters move across flat backgrounds. With skill, artists can make things appear solid using careful shading, colouring, and **perspective** techniques. However, many of today's animators work in three dimensions. Computer animation in 3D is a bit like stop motion clay animation. Virtual characters are built or "sculpted" using programming so that they can be viewed from all sides and move through 3D backgrounds.

Virtual sculpture

The first step in **3D computer animation** is to create a **virtual stick model**, just like the wire skeletons or armatures used in stop motion animation. Animators define every part of a stick model with coordinates that they key into the computer. For example, a stick model of a human arm will have coordinates for the shoulder, elbow, wrist, and finger joints.

Next the animator programs in **avars**. These are commands that control how the different parts of the stick model move, such as how far a jaw can open. The more avars, the more realistically a character moves. For example, Woody, one of the main characters in *Toy Story*, had 700 avars.

In human faces, hundreds of muscles create expressions. *Toy Story* animators programmed over 100 avars in Woody's face to make his expressions appear realistic.

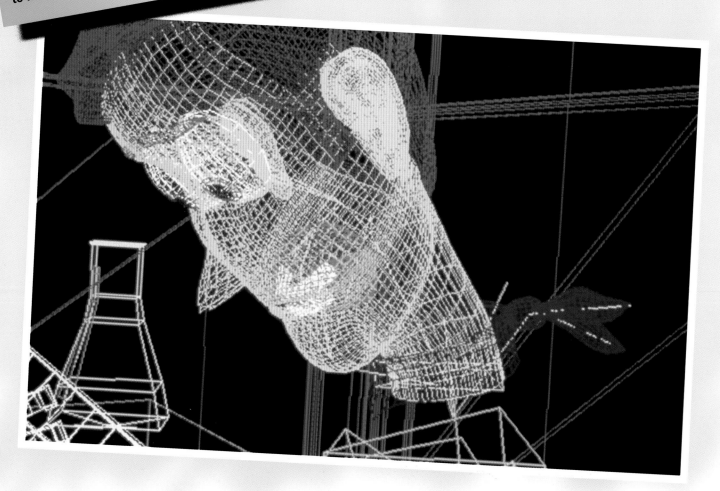

Computer animators create the outer shape of a character using a "mesh" attached to the virtual stick model. The mesh is a grid of mini-shapes such as triangles and squares, a bit like virtual chicken wire, also defined by coordinates. The arrangement of the mesh may change as the stick model moves. The mesh plus the stick model together form a virtual **wire frame model**.

Painting by numbers

Very few things look like mesh, so the next step is to add colour, texture, and surface detail. In simple terms, it is rather like wallpapering over the mesh. The wallpaper can look like skin, metal, wood, or whatever the animated object is supposed to look like.

If you have ever painted on a computer, you know it takes time. **Rendering** is the word for when the computer paints in a mesh automatically, dot by dot, following its programming. Accurate rendering can make surfaces appear rough, smooth, dull, or shiny.

The wire frame model of Woody was rendered to cover it with flesh, hair, and clothing.

Powerful business

Rendering takes lots of computer power. To create a full-length animation film on an average home computer would take many years. Modern animation studios have "render farms" of lots of powerful computers connected together.

Getting the idea

Before animators start to draw or program, it is vital to plan animation projects fully. The planning stage is usually called **pre-production** and starts with an idea.

What's your story?

Imagine the lives of a strange cartoon family with a lazy father who obsesses about doughnuts, a worrisome mother with very tall blue hair, a trouble-making son, a daughter brighter than the adults, and a very resilient baby. Recognize *The Simpsons* from this? Their inventor, Matt Groening, got the names for the characters from his own family and some of their character traits from people he knew when he was young. Animators often incorporate bits of their own life experiences into their stories. But autobiography is just one of many possible sources of inspiration.

Inspired

Here are a few of the sources that have inspired animators:

● *the classics:* some animators are inspired by well-known stories from plays, novels, and short stories. They may follow the original closely, as in Stanislav Sokolov's stop motion films *Shakespeare: The Animated Tales*. However, sometimes adaptations are rather different from the originals. For example, Disney's *The Jungle Book* was only loosely based on the stories about Mowgli in Rudyard Kipling's *The Jungle Book*.

Scooby Doo was inspired by a radio show about detectives roaming the world solving mysteries and a TV show about a scatterbrained teenager and his friends.

- *fairy tales and myths:* many animators have been inspired by popular folk tales featuring mythical creatures such as fairies, wizards, and goblins. Examples include Disney's *Aladdin* and *Sleeping Beauty*. DreamWorks' *Shrek* used bits from many different fairy tales to hilarious effect.

- *recent events:* animators, like many other artists, respond to what is happening in the world around them. A good example is Tex Avery's short animated film *Blitz Wolf*, made in 1942, during World War II. The film depicts Adolf Hitler as a wolf and the Allied forces as three little pigs.

- *remakes:* some ideas are too good to use just once. The most famous remake of recent years was Disney's *The Lion King*, which closely followed a Japanese cartoon called *Jungle Taitei*.

The right format

The length and scope of a story depends partly on where it will be shown. Some different formats include kids' TV animation serials, animated music videos, animation for mobile phone screens, animated film title sequences, and web animation. For some of these formats a simple, good idea is all that is needed, but others require long, involved stories featuring many characters.

Shrek 2 put a new spin on ideas from different classic fairy tales, including a heroic ogre and a sword-fighting Puss-in-Boots.

Scripts

Getting an idea for a story is one thing, but how do animators present their ideas so they can be turned into animations? A **script** is a way of changing the idea into a clear sequence of events involving different characters.

A synopsis

The first step in creating a script is to write a short, simple **synopsis** of the story. This involves jotting down some notes about each character, such as what they wear or look like, how they move, or what their skills are.

Scenes

The next step is to break up the story into chunks and write the script in **scenes**. A scene is a section of action with a particular setting and particular characters. Scenes fit together to tell a whole story. For each scene, the script describes the setting and lists the characters involved. It also describes what happens in the action and who says what to whom. It helps to write down **dialogue** and action on separate lines so they do not get mixed up.

Storyboarding

Storyboarding is a very important part of all film-making. A **storyboard** is a rough sketch plan that looks a bit like a giant comic strip. It illustrates sequences of action, sketched within boxes to help the animator picture the look of each scene. The sketches show rough outlines rather than finished drawings, often in pencil.

When creating storyboards, animators work out how long each scene or sequence needs to be to show the action. They start to plan the scenes frame-by-frame.

Here are a few things animators need to consider when they create storyboards for each scene or sequence:

- *viewpoint:* will the action in the scene be viewed from above or below, close up, or at a distance?

- *movement:* what is still, what is moving and if something is moving, is it moving quickly or slowly?

- *lighting:* is the action taking place in the dark or is the scene brightly lit? If it is brightly lit, is the light natural or artificial?

How many scenes do you need?

Answer: enough to tell the story. For example, imagine one scene showing a character mixing cake ingredients and another showing them eating the cake at a picnic. You don't need to include scenes showing the cake baking or the journey to the picnic spot because viewers will fill in the gaps in the story in their minds. This means less time needs to be spent animating less significant action.

Chris Wedge, **director** of *Ice Age* and *Robots*, adjusts the frames to find the best order of action within each scene and get the storyboard right.

Sketching characters

Storyboard sketches may show characters as little more than stick people. But it helps in planning action to make them look a bit like the actual characters you have imagined. Animators usually sketch characters as simple cartoons.

Cartoon faces, such as Homer Simpson's, have large eyes that can easily show emotion, even if they are not very realistic. Cartoon characters often have unusual bodily proportions to remind viewers of what they can and cannot do. For example, strong but slightly unintelligent characters are often heavily built with small heads.

Getting it right

In animation studios a lot of time is taken to make a clear, finished storyboard. After all, animation is a very lengthy process and expensive to film, so it is a waste of time and money if the storyboard is wrong. The director of an animated film will make sure the lengths of different scenes work well together at storyboard stage. For example, they need the right balance between showing exciting action and the less exciting bits that establish what characters are like.

Cutting scenes

Any frames that are not helping the story progress may be discarded. Special effects in animation are often quite expensive to create. Depending on how much money they have to make their film, directors may decide to cut scenes that look as if they will be expensive to film.

Animatics

Once finished, each frame of the final storyboard is photographed. Together these frames make up a rough film called the Leica Reel or **animatic**. This is the reference that animators work from to create final frames. Each finished frame replaces the reference frame as it is done, so the animatic is constantly updated.

This storyboard frame from *The Corpse Bride* is a pencil sketch that visualizes the story script.

40.1272

Try it yourself

Why not create a storyboard using 12 frames? In the first frame, show a character walking towards a creepy looking house. In the last frame, show a close-up of a screaming mouth. What is going to happen in-between in your story? Who is screaming and why? How many characters are there and is there any dialogue?

Write a script before you start on the storyboard. The story can have up to three scenes or sequences of action. Draw your storyboard on a large sheet of paper with three rows of four boxes, one row for each scene.

Bringing ideas to life

Once all the ideas are in place, it is time to animate. This stage in the process is called **production**. The aim of production is to make characters act believably in their worlds. Animators make this happen by adding sounds, movement, and backgrounds.

Recording sound

When you watch the average home video, the wobbly filming is accompanied by the voices of the people in the video, the voice of the cameraperson, and any background sounds such as planes that happen to be flying over as the video is being filmed. In these cases, the sounds and images are recorded at the same time.

Recording for animation

In animation, sounds cannot be recorded at the same time as filming, frame-by-frame, because the sounds would sound wrong when played at 24 frames per second. Therefore, sounds are recorded separately and usually before any animation has begun.

Dialogue

One of the great things about animation is that your characters can use any voice you like. You need to find someone with a voice that you think fits the character and then use a microphone and sound recorder to capture them speaking the words in your script. When several characters are talking to each other in a scene, the different voices are recorded at the same time to make conversations sound natural.

A clear recording

Directors of animated films generally use actors who can speak clearly and sometimes with different voices and accents. Once the best recorded version is ready, the director adds the dialogue digitally to the animatic. They may add or remove frames to synchronize words and planned action better.

Sound effects

Most of the noise we hear in everyday life is not dialogue. We are surrounded by sounds all the time, from the hum of a computer that we rarely notice, to startling bangs and crashes. Sound details make animation more realistic. Often animators can simply record sounds around them, such as a car engine or breaking glass. However, animation studios create many small sounds, from rustling paper to creaking robot joints, using **foley artists**. For example, foley artists may walk or run on boxes containing gravel or on wooden floorboards to create the sound of different footsteps.

Actress Jada Pinkett Smith adds dialogue for the character Gloria the Hippo in DreamWorks' 2005 film *Madagascar*.

Tricks of the trade

Real sounds such as birdsong sometimes appear odd in invented worlds populated by cartoon characters. For Nick Park's *The Wrong Trousers*, featuring Wallace and Gromit and a criminal penguin, a foley artist slapped his thighs to create the sound of the penguin's feet rather than record a real penguin walking. The invented sound suited the Plasticine feet better than the real sound.

Making frames

When the dialogue and sound effects are in place on the animatic, artists and modellers can start to draw, make, or position their characters for each frame. In most animation studios, there are two types of animator – **keyframers** and **tweeners**.

Keyframers

Keyframers or key animators create the key or most important frames in a scene to get across the main points of the action. They also create drawings showing how the characters look from various angles and in various poses based on rough guides in the storyboard. They define the range of possible movements for each character so they do things consistently throughout the animation.

Tweeners

Tweeners or assistant animators are trained to be copycats. They fill in the missing frames in the style of the keyframer and fill in any character details the keyframer has left out. If you plan to animate on your own, you will have to be both keyframer and tweener!

Lip-synch

When we are talking or listening to people we almost always look into their faces. Subconsciously we are seeing how tiny movements in their face muscles fit in with what they are saying, and how the look of their face expresses their mood. A basic part of animation is fitting characters' mouth shapes to recorded dialogue so characters look as if they are really talking. This is called **lip-synch**.

Facial expression capture

Animators often model face shapes by copying the facial expressions of actors. However, they also use "facial expression capture". This is when actors perform wearing special sensors all over their faces. As they change their facial expressions, the motion of the sensors is filmed using sensitive cameras.

The film is then digitized and used as the basis for accurate wire frame computer models of faces that move just like the faces of the actors.

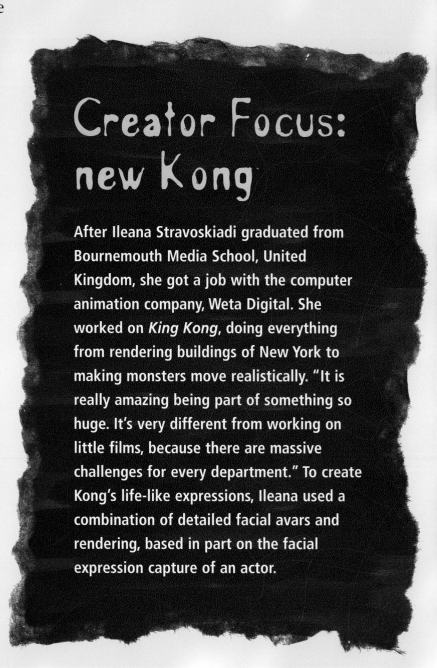

Creator Focus: new Kong

After Ileana Stravoskiadi graduated from Bournemouth Media School, United Kingdom, she got a job with the computer animation company, Weta Digital. She worked on *King Kong*, doing everything from rendering buildings of New York to making monsters move realistically. "It is really amazing being part of something so huge. It's very different from working on little films, because there are massive challenges for every department." To create Kong's life-like expressions, Ileana used a combination of detailed facial avars and rendering, based in part on the facial expression capture of an actor.

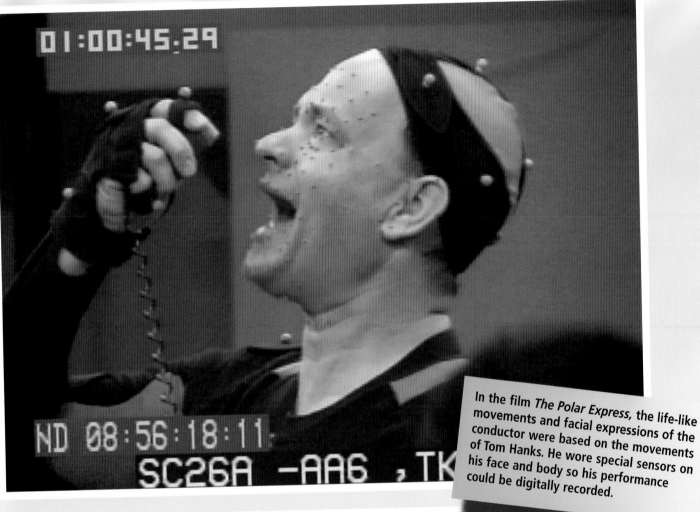

01:00:45:29

ND 08:56:18:11

SC26A -AA6 ,TK

In the film *The Polar Express,* the life-like movements and facial expressions of the conductor were based on the movements of Tom Hanks. He wore special sensors on his face and body so his performance could be digitally recorded.

Creator feature: Nick Park

Animator Nick Park is a famous creator of stop motion animations, including films featuring Wallace and Gromit. Wallace is a cheese-loving inventor and Gromit his smart, silent dog. Park's short films *The Wrong Trousers* and *A Close Shave* both won Oscars and worldwide acclaim. The feature-length film *Wallace and Gromit: The Curse of the Were-Rabbit* won an Oscar for Best Animated Feature in 2006.

Claytime

Park animates using clay similar to Plasticine. He says it gives an "organic, subtle human feel" to his characters that audiences like. He first used this medium because it was much cheaper to buy than cels to make cartoons. Now, even though he could choose any medium, Park still prefers clay animation to any other. He believes it gives a hand-crafted feel to his films. In close-up shots, you can even spot fingerprints on the clay!

Man and talking cat?

Park first created the characters Wallace and Gromit when he was at art school, long before he was a famous animator. At first, Gromit was a cat! When he was a student at film college, Nick decided to start *A Grand Day Out*, a film about someone building a rocket in his basement and going to the moon to find cheese. At the script stage he decided Wallace could be the inventor, but that Gromit needed to become a dog. He said this was because: "A dog would be chunkier and larger, and easier to work with in clay."

Park had already recorded the dialogue for Gromit when he realized that the dog did not need a voice to have an interesting character. In one scene, Gromit supports a door that Wallace is sawing into pieces to make the rocket. Gromit could not move because he was holding the door, so Park just animated his ears, eyebrows, and head. After watching the film, he saw that he could "get such a lot of character from just those little movements".

Mouth swap

Nick Park does not completely remodel the whole of Wallace's head for each frame during lip-synch. He simply takes off one mouth and sticks on another with a different shape. Each mouth shape looks as if it makes a different sound. For example, the word "cheese" requires the "ch", "eeee", and "se".

Nick Park finds it is easier to animate large models of Wallace and Gromit. Any smaller than this and it is too fiddly to adjust model positions between frames.

Keeping movement real

Animators have tried many methods to make movement seem more real. For example, **rotoscoping** used in traditional cel animation, such as Disney's *Snow White and the Seven Dwarfs*, involved filming moving actors and then tracing their outlines on to cels.

Motion capture is when actors wear dark suits with white dots or ping-pong balls stuck on at important points, such as their joints. An array of cameras in different positions films the dots as the actors go through their moves. Software converts the position of the dots into digital wire frames that can be used to make characters move naturally.

Rotoscoping allowed new levels of realism in animated characters such as Snow White in the 1930s.

More than real

Real movements are often small and complex. They are also subtle and in danger of being missed by the audience. Movement in cartoons is therefore usually exaggerated to make it more obvious to the viewer what is happening. Here are a few of the tricks that animators use to exaggerate reality:

● *pose*: animators hold a character's pose for several frames instead of making each frame very different to the last. Slight changes between frames, for example in eyes or hands, help show the character's emotions. A great example is when a character such as Daffy Duck hangs in mid air before falling.

● *anticipation*: animators often include more frames showing the anticipation of an action than the action itself. This helps prepare the audience for what is about to happen. For example, to show a character pitching a ball, an animator may include more frames showing the character pulling their arm back in preparation, than frames showing the ball being pitched.

● *keep moving*: animators often exaggerate the way we keep moving after stopping. For example, if you put your brakes on suddenly when cycling, you carry on moving forward even though the bike has stopped.

Thoughtful characters

Imagine you are sneaking up quietly to surprise a friend. Part of what we would see is your creeping movement, but part would be the look of concentration as you try to remain unnoticed. For animation to appear life-like, every movement or action of a character must appear to be the result of what they are thinking. One simple way to achieve this is to move the eyes or head in the direction of the next action. For example, a custard pie is flying towards a character's face, so they look or turn towards it to communicate "I know what's going to happen" before it hits the target.

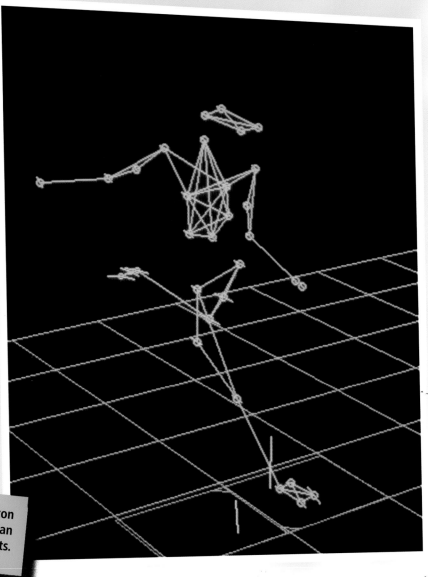

Each dot on this wire frame skeleton was created using motion capture of an actor's movements.

In the background

An animated character can be engaging without any background to perform in front of. However, a believable background sets the scene for what characters can and cannot do. In early cel animation, background artists painted backgrounds by hand but today they create them using computer software.

Artists may scan and modify existing photographs or other images, or draw the backgrounds from scratch. They can edit colours and shapes on-screen. The backgrounds used in stop motion animation are rather like mini-sets for actors, containing model buildings, plants, and other objects made to the right scale for the character models.

For this scene from *The Jungle Book*, animators painted a jungle background and used overlaid cels to animate not only the characters but also the moving river and the foreground trees.

Background artists often use traditional painting techniques to make 2D cartoons look three-dimensional. For example, perspective is the way that things appear to be smaller when further away and **foreshortening** is the way we draw the nearest part of an object bigger so that the rest of it appears to lie flat or recede into the distance. Another technique is to make the furthest background blurred or lighter in colour so it highlights what is happening closer to the viewer.

Real and imagined worlds

Animators use all kinds of sources to make backgrounds look real – for example, detailed architectural plans or models, objects in museums, car catalogues, or Internet images. They may also create totally made-up worlds, but these need to have some recognizable features so viewers might imagine themselves in that space.

Background artists sometimes make backgrounds look unreal for effect. For example, in the first cartoons of the *Road Runner and Wile E. Coyote* series the desert backgrounds were copied from real desert photographs. As the series went on, the backgrounds got simpler and more distorted, with odd unstable-looking rock formations and bright yellow skies. The animators knew by then that the action of their characters was the important bit and the background only had to suggest vaguely the desert world as a space the characters moved through.

Try it yourself

Try painting a background. First use a soft pencil to draw basic outlines of mountains in the distance. Paint the mountains with diluted grey and violet watercolours. While the paint is still wet use a dry brush to blend the colours together. Use a similar technique for blue and white in the sky.

Let these colours dry and then start to add more detailed middle ground elements such as trees or buildings – remember that these will be quite small as they are not close up. Finally add foreground elements in bright colours such as rocks, a path, or tufts of grass.

Light

Lighting makes a big difference to backgrounds. For example, animators might use dim light to make things appear mysterious. In 3D computer animation, lighting effects such as shadows and reflections are rendered on-screen. In stop motion animation, some lighting, such as the light from street lamps, is built into the background sets, but some lighting is added from outside the set. If you plan to shoot stop motion, it is important to check the lighting is from the same direction for each frame in a sequence or scene. Otherwise you may get unwanted shadows appearing in your film.

Animation style

The look or feel of any animation project is a combination of many things, such as how realistically the characters move and the details of the world they inhabit. Animation style is also determined by the choice of medium. For example, the animators of *The Snowman* cartoon created frames in the soft style of the coloured pencil drawings of Raymond Briggs' original book. Style is also partly to do with the colours or lighting used. For example, Evan Cagle gave a gloomy, 19th-century etching feel to his cartoon *Honey* by using dim lighting, lots of shadow, and a dull colour palette.

The Corpse Bride uses a unique animation style to tell a story ranging from the land of the dead to the land of the living.

With 3D animation techniques such as motion capture and powerful rendering, it is possible to create characters and backgrounds that look real. However, this requires very powerful computers and complex software. Many animators choose to create a realistic style, for example the texture of cloth, by photographing stop motion models than by constructing them digitally on-screen.

Some animators like their work to look older than it really is. For example, characters in the film *The Iron Giant* were created using 3D animation but made to look more two dimensional using cel-shading software. This converts the gradual shading on characters, caused by virtual light falling on their surfaces, to just one or two separate tones and adds black outlines around the characters.

The Corpse Bride

Skeleton dogs and horses, tall hats, dark rings around the eyes, and candle-lit, cobwebbed interiors … The style of director Tim Burton's 2005 stop motion film is very distinctive. The world of *The Corpse Bride* looks jagged, old, drab, and dying but it is made in a very modern way. For example, the characters may look like traditional puppets but they are actually state-of-the-art stainless steel armatures, cloaked in foam, whose poses and expressions can be changed using electronically operated gears hidden inside.

Double-frames

Animators try all sorts of shortcuts to save time as they create their work. The most common is probably shooting in double-frame. This means photographing each image twice so two adjacent frames are exactly the same. The advantage is that for 24 frames-per-second film, you only have to make 12 different images for each second. And the finished result is not noticeably jerkier than single-frame.

Repeat showings

Animators repeat all sorts of things from sound effects and backgrounds to particular animation sequences such as running or walking. These repeat sequences are called **animation loops**. They were commonly used in TV cartoon series from the 1960s onwards, such as *Deputy Dawg*.

You've probably seen the opening sequences of each episode of *The Simpsons*. Most of it is repeated each episode but some bits change a little. For example, Bart writes a different message on the chalk board each time. These changes keep the humour fresh and have become part of the individual style of the programme.

Helpful programming

In 3D animation, with the right programming, computers can cut down on the work involved in creating backgrounds. For example, for his film *KAZE Ghost Warrior*, Timothy Albee got the computer to make some backgrounds itself. To create a bamboo forest, Albee programmed the computer to draw one bamboo plant, then draw other near identical, but different sized plants randomly positioned within a background space. This enabled him quickly to create a background showing thousands of bamboo plants.

The start of each of *The Simpsons* episode is mostly an animation loop, until the family sit on the sofa.

38

This frame shows Yugi, from the animated film *Yu-Gi-Oh!* Yugi is a typical anime character with big, expressive eyes.

Creator focus: Osamu Tezuka and limited animation

Osamu Tezuka was a major Japanese comic creator who wanted to make anime (cartoons) versions of his manga (comics) quickly by drawing fewer cels than usual. So he came up with the idea of limited animation. He formed a library of cels showing characters with typical expressions and poses that could be used again and again in different anime. Limited animation allowed many elements in Tezuka's animation to be repeated. For example, Astro Boy, his first animated character, was often shown flying at the same angle and in the same direction against the same background. Tezuka's time-saving method spread across Japan and to other countries. Around the world animators began to use limited animation and even to mimic Tezuka's style of drawing.

Bringing it all together

At the end of filming, an animator should have an animatic composed of fantastic-looking finished frames. It will have a soundtrack of sound effects and dialogue. Now begins the process of **post-production** – enhancing and editing to get a final version ready to show to the public.

Being effective

Special effects are moving elements added to films that would be difficult or expensive to create at the time of filming. For example, it would be too destructive and expensive to actually blow up a building, so an effect to suggest an explosion is added. In the past, animated special effects such as rushing water, flames, or smoke were painted or photographed on to frames. For example, for scenes in Disney's *Fantasia*, animators overlaid film of real rain, shot against a dark background, on the animatic.

Stop motion special effects are difficult to create. Moving flames, smoke, and substances such as water cannot be held still, photographed, and then slightly changed in position between frames. Therefore, other substances are used, such as crinkled cellophane for water or cotton wool for smoke. Animators have to be ingenious. For example, in Nick Park's *A Close Shave,* the foamy water Gromit uses to wash windows with is actually white hair wax with shiny glass beads in it!

Some special effects created by substitutions do not look very realistic. Today, special effects are mostly added to animation on-screen during post-production. These special effects are called **CGI** or computer-generated image effects. Computer programs can add swirling mist and digital light effects such as reflections off shiny surfaces. They can even bend or angle background features to stress the movement of characters in front of them.

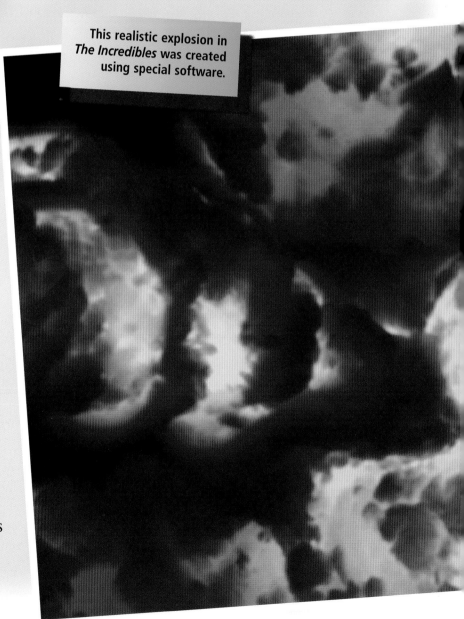

This realistic explosion in *The Incredibles* was created using special software.

Tricks of the trade

In comics, artists can suggest speedy movement of characters by drawing **motion lines**. In stop motion animation, animators can suggest speed by blurring backgrounds. During the train chase sequence in *The Wrong Trousers*, Nick Park photographed individual frames of the train as it was moving along a short stretch of track. He moved the camera exactly in time with the train. This meant the train and characters were sharply in focus but the background appeared blurred.

Dancing zebras flank a lion cub singing "Oh I just can't wait to be king". This is one of many musical scenes from *The Lion King* animated to fit a recording of a song.

Theme time

Music can set the mood for any animated film sequence, from exciting or mysterious to sad or happy. Some animated films use music as a starting point in the pre-production stage. For example, the aim of Disney's *Fantasia* was to animate characters and scenes based on famous pieces of classical music. But most animation music is added post-production.

Animation directors use film composers to write musical themes. Usually, directors have an idea of the sort of theme or sound they want. Composers then write music specifically for each second of the animatic. Some find cues or points in the action to help them write music. They might then introduce a particular tune when a main character appears. Others watch scenes and compose themes to fit the mood.

Fine tuning

Using keyboards, composers can try out different combinations of instrument sounds for the basic theme to see what sounds best. For example, the African vocals and drums suit the setting and characters in Disney's *The Lion King*. Composers then orchestrate the music, which means they write out accurate music for each different instrument involved. The final step, once the theme is approved by the director, is to record it in a recording studio. Usually, professional musicians are hired for this.

This animated title featuring Bugs Bunny preceded many madcap Warner Brothers' cartoons from the 1950s onwards.

Titles

You sit down in the cinema, the lights dim, and the film begins. The first thing you see is not the main animation but the title sequence showing the name of the animation and who made it. You may have seen older cartoons such as *Looney Tunes* that always start with the Warner Brothers' logo. The letters in the title words are often animated, perhaps moving across the screen, expanding, or jostling for position with each other. The letter style used helps make the film recognizable and may give an idea of the film content. For example, the letters making up "Bug's" in Disney's *A Bug's Life* had bug-shapes cut into them.

Try it yourself

A film called *The Banana* could be about several different things. For example, it could be about a fruit that makes the difference between an athlete winning and losing a race, or it could be about a giant yellow spaceship threatening the Earth. Try to come up with four different styles of title for *The Banana*, each representing a different film story. For example, a science fiction version might have futuristic letters with aliens hiding behind them. You can do this on a computer using the computer **fonts** or you can draw the letters.

43

Chopping and changing

Most animatics at the post-production stage should be very close to being a finished film. But however carefully an animation has been planned, frame-by-frame, sometimes things need to be changed. This is the job of the **editor**. Maybe after watching the whole film the balance of scene lengths needs to be adjusted. In the early days of animation, film editors required skill with a knife and sticky tape! If a frame or sequence needed to be removed, the editor would cut it out and stick the other bits back together in the right order.

Today, all animation editing is done on-screen using special software such as *Avid* or *Final Cut Pro*. The first step is to convert the animatic into digital clips. The clips are then dragged using a mouse on to a timeline representing the length of the film. Using the software, the editor can easily move the clips or shorten them before deciding on the best order and length.

Film editors complete the appearance of animation frames on-screen by digitally adjusting colours and lighting.

The right combination

The final process in animation is to create a finished piece. If frames are removed or the order of frames changed, editors will also need to adjust the dialogue, sound effects, music, and special effects. For example, they may change the mix of music or adjust the lighting used in digital special effects to those in the filmed frames they fit into. Once everything is just as the director wants, the different elements are combined into a finished digital version. This can then be output to film to show in cinemas or other formats.

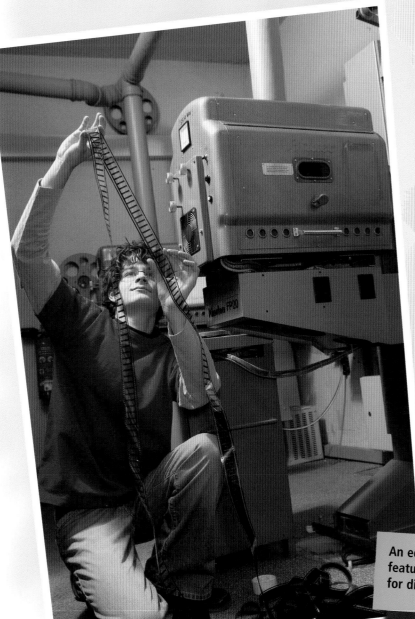

An edited and completed animated feature film is loaded on to a projector for display on a cinema screen.

Finding the audience

Large-scale animation feature films take a long time to create and involve a lot of people, so they cost a lot of money to make. That means it is vital to promote, publicise, and market the films to ensure people come to see them. This is the job of the publicity and marketing department and they get to work before the pre-production stage begins. In this way they can generate interest in and money for the project.

Merchandising

Publicity often involves the creation of original artwork for items such as posters, stickers, books, and board games, which often become available before a film is first shown in cinemas. Toy models of characters are often sold or given out as free gifts with cereals or fast food meals. Publicists may also collaborate with video game makers to develop new games featuring animated characters from a film.

All these forms of marketing are types of **merchandising**. A successful Hollywood film can make over £60 million from the box office takings, while merchandising can add another £25–100 million!

Previews

Publicity departments also use short, key sections of the animation in previews shown on cinema, television, and in pop-up computer advertisements. In Japan, pictures of cartoon characters are sometimes sent to people's mobile phones so they can be tested for popularity with the public.

One way publicists increase the interest in animated films before they are finished is by sending images of characters to mobile phones.

Show and tell

For independent or new animators, one way to get a film seen is to post it on the Internet or on your own website. Some people take their animation shorts to animation film festivals. This is a great opportunity to show work to audiences for feedback.

And on rare occasions new animators are talent-spotted at festivals by animation companies. At animation festivals you might also see a new film by a more famous animator. For example, the first public showing of Nick Park's stop motion film *A Close Shave* was at a festival in 1997.

Creator focus: Matt Groening and The Simpsons

Matt Groening's *The Simpsons* began in 1986 as short cartoon episodes that appeared as part of another comedy show. Since then it has become the most popular TV show in the world and the longest running comedy in TV history. The cartoon characters Homer, Bart, Marge, Lisa, and Maggie Simpson appeal to all ages. Their simple, easily recognizable features are easy to reproduce and appear on mugs, wristwatches, puzzles, T-shirts, beach balls, board games, and many other forms of merchandise across the world.

The US TV channel Fox painted Marge and other Simpsons characters on an aeroplane to promote its TV show.

Getting into animation

Do you want to turn an idea into an all-singing, all-dancing animation? Have you got the patience to make a stop motion film? Want to perfect your lip-synch? Becoming an animator could be your future.

Improve the basics

Whatever complex computer software you may eventually learn how to use for your animations, you will need to be a good artist.

To help develop your skills, get yourself a sketchbook and pencil, or some modelling clay, and practise as much as you can.

Here are some ideas:

● *anatomy:* visit a natural history museum or zoo and copy the skeletons and forms of people and animals. How do they change shape when they move?

● *thinking in 3D:* draw things from different viewpoints with different lighting, using shading. How do things look different from different angles? Sculpt some 3D models out of clay.

● *composition:* look at paintings and photographs to see how artists have arranged elements in the foreground against backgrounds. Draw characters on tracing paper and test out composition on different backgrounds.

Try it yourself

Lego animation is very popular. A quick search on the Internet reveals a lot of examples – there are even Brickmation film festivals! It is easy to do at home if you have a Lego set, a digital camera, and a tripod. Start with your idea, write a script, and then create a storyboard.

Extend what you know

If you like animation you will already appreciate films and TV cartoons. Now start to study it. For example, get a video or DVD of a film and watch scenes or sequences at slow speed, ideally frame-by-frame to check out the composition. Make notes or sketches about what is in the background, how animators show movement, the lighting, colours used, and backgrounds. Think about how the characters are animated to look as if they are thinking before they act. Visit animation displays at museums and galleries or animation festivals. Why not set up an animation club at school? You can share ideas, equipment, and talents to create shared animation projects.

Sculpting in clay is ideal practice for understanding 3D shapes, especially if you want to get into stop motion animation.

Construct a background, place your characters in their starting positions, and start filming frame-by-frame. Once you have your frames, you could load them into software such as *Stop Motion Maker*. Finish off the film by adding sound effects and dialogue, special effects, and titles.

Lego figures are ideal for animation. They have few moving parts, they are easy to pose, and they can be accurately placed on studded Lego boards and brick backgrounds.

Going further

You have practised as much as you can and you are still very keen to animate. One of the best ways to improve your skills is to enrol in an art college or university. You can study general art or specialize in animation right from the start. This will give you the opportunity to use the latest equipment and software. You may have classes in creating scripts and making better storyboards. You may be able to try out motion capture and avar programming. The end point of many courses is to put together some carefully planned and finished animations to prove your technical skills.

Proof perfect

The "Try it yourself" exercises throughout this book can be a starting point for your portfolio. It is important to include supporting material showing, for example, how you developed the projects from idea to storyboard, what affected your choice of medium, and any technical challenges you faced. The most important part of your portfolio is a **showreel**. This is a collection of finished sequences or even short films that prove you can animate. Most showreels include walking, stretching, and squashing movements, which are common to many animated creations.

The different workers in Pixar's animation studio share office space with many colourful things including models of familiar cartoon characters.

Case study: Chris Collins, animation student

Chris is studying 3D computer animation at college. He is doing the course "to gain the ability of creating high quality skeletons and muscle patterns" to create more convincing characters. Going to college has given him access to much more powerful computers and advanced animation software than he would have access to at school or home. The college also runs an annual animation week where people from major companies come to find new animators to work for them.

Chris recommends that you study art through school: "They tell art students at my college to never put a pencil and paper down. We have to constantly be creating and drawing new characters so that they may be of use further on into the course."

Getting out there

Animators are in demand. Educators, advertisers, film studios, websites, and video game developers all employ people with animation skills. In a large animation studio there are many specific jobs, from storyboard artists and model makers to CGI computer technicians and editors.

Through your studies you will probably have discovered your strengths. Even if you cannot get that dream job in a studio straight away, keep updating your animating skills and maybe one day your work will be appreciated by others and animation will become your career.

Glossary

2D having two dimensions – width and height. When something is 2D, it has no depth and looks flat.

3D having three dimensions – width, height, and depth. 3D is short for "three dimensional". When something is painted so it looks 3D, it looks solid, not flat.

3D computer animation animation using images generated on computers in a virtual three-dimensional space

acetate transparent plastic material

animatic filmed version of a storyboard

animation loop animation sequence or scene that is repeated or reused

armature rigid, often wire, framework or skeleton that supports an outer body of Plasticine or other soft sculpting material

avars commands an animator uses to control how the parts of a virtual stick model move

cel transparent plastic sheet that can be drawn on and then overlaid in layers

CGI (computer generated imagery) film sequence generated by computers

dialogue conversation between characters in a film

director person who directs or controls the making of a film

editor person who makes sure a film flows well from scene to scene

feature length full-length

flickbook book with slightly different images on each page that give the illusion of a moving cartoon when you flick through the pages quickly

foley artist sound effects artist who creates and records sound effects for a film

font style of lettering

foreshortening when the nearest parts of an object are drawn bigger so that the rest of the object looks as if it is further away

frame single image or picture within a sequence of images that is part of an animation or other film

graphics tablet alternative to a computer mouse. You move a digitized stylus over a small board to write or draw on-screen.

illusion when something appears to be happening or there when it really is not

keyframer key animator who creates the final, complete version of how a character looks

lip-synch make lip movements in a film correspond exactly to the sounds they are supposed to be making

merchandising producing toys and other goods, such as sticker books, that are linked to a film

morphing (sometimes called tweening) process of generating intermediate shapes between different key frames

motion capture when actors' movements are filmed, digitized, and used to create similar movements in animated characters

motion lines drawn lines that suggest movement

persistence of vision way that an image is stored by the brain for a split second. This creates an illusion of continuous motion when sequences of different images are viewed at speed.

perspective appearance of objects or people relative to one another as determined by their distance from the viewer

portfolio collection of pieces of creative work to show to potential employers or educators

post-production period during which all the production work is done after the main film footage and sound effects have been finished

praxinoscope animation device invented in 1877 by Emile Reynaud. It used a strip of pictures inside a spinning cylinder and mirrors to project the images on to a screen.

pre-production period during which all the work on a film is done before the image, sound, and other work begins

production period during which the main animation work is done on a film, including the film footage and sound effects

registration putting two or more images together so that they are perfectly aligned. This makes the final image well defined.

rendering when a computer program turns an outline image into a fully-formed, 3D image, by adding colours and shading

rotoscoping technique used in animation where the movements of live actors are filmed and then their outlines are traced on to cels

scene set of actions or dialogue that take place in one location and at one time in a film or story

script detailed written description of a story that includes scene-by-scene dialogue, instructions for directors, and instructions on how to represent the action

showreel collection of a person's animation films and sequences that demonstrate their technical abilities

special effects visual effects used in films to create effects that cannot be achieved by normal techniques, such as showing someone in outer space

stop motion animation in which objects are photographed frame-by-frame and altered slightly in between each frame

storyboard series of sketches showing the plot, action, characters, and setting of a film, made before filming begins

synopsis short summary of a story or script

tweener assistant animator who copies the style of keyframers to fill in frames

virtual formed on a computer

virtual stick model model that looks like a wire model, but is formed on a computer screen

wire frame model virtual stick model on-screen that is covered in a mesh that looks like chicken wire

zoetrope device that produces an illusion of movement using a quick succession of still images viewed through a slot in a rotating drum

Find out more

Animated films

There are hundreds of animated films to choose from but here are some of the greats you will be able to see:

Aardman:
A Grand Day Out (1989)
The Wrong Trousers (1993)
A Close Shave (1995)
Chicken Run (2000)
Wallace and Gromit: The Curse of the Were-Rabbit (2005)

Tim Burton:
The Nightmare Before Christmas (1999)
The Corpse Bride (2005)

Sylvain Chomet:
Belleville Rendezvous/The Triplets of Belleville (2003)

Disney:
Snow White and The Seven Dwarfs (1937)
Fantasia (1940)
Pinocchio (1940)
101 Dalmations (1961)
The Jungle Book (1967)
Who Framed Roger Rabbit? (1988) (interesting mix of animation and real-life film)
Aladdin (1992)

DreamWorks Animation:
Shrek/Shrek 2 (2001/2004)
Madagascar (2005)

Miyazaki:
Princess Mononoke (1997)
Spirited Away (2002)
Howl's Moving Castle (2005)

Pixar Animation Studios:
Toy Story/Toy Story 2 (1995/1999)
Monsters Inc. (2001)
Ice Age (2002)
Finding Nemo (2003)
The Incredibles (2004)
Cars (2006)

Books

Animation: From Script to Screen, by Shamus Culhane (Saint Martin's Press, 1990)

Flash Cartoon Animation: Learn from the Pros, by Glenn Kirkpatrick and Kevin Peaty (Friends of ED, 2003)

Cracking Animation: The Aardman Book of 3-D Animation, by Peter Lord and Brian Sibley (Thames and Hudson, 2004)

Character Animation in 3D: Use Traditional Drawing Techniques to Produce Stunning CGI Animation (*Visual Effects & Animation* series), by Steve Roberts (Focal Press, 2004)

Stop Motion: Craft Skills for Model Animation, by Susannah Shaw (Focal Press, 2003)

Facial Expressions: A Visual Reference for Artists, by Mark Simon (Watson-Guptill, 2005)

Making an Animated Film: A Practical Guide, by Matt West (The Crowood Press, 2005)

The Animator's Survival Kit: A Working Manual of Methods, Principles and Formulas for Computer, Stop-Motion, Games and Classical Animators, by Richard Williams (Faber and Faber, 2002)

Software

MotionArtist 3.0 (efrontier)
Create Flash animation using built-in elements and by adding your own sound effects and images.

Stop Motion Maker (Shareit)
Look at the screengrabs of stop motion animation techniques at:
http://www.stopmotionmaker.com/index.html

ToonBoomStudio (toonboom)
Visit http://www.toonboom.com/products to download trial software, view tutorials, and showcase examples of animations made using ToonBoom.

Websites

http://www.aardman.com
The website of the Aardman studio, creators of the stop motion films featuring Wallace and Gromit. The site includes clips of Aardman's films and advertisements.

http://www.animationmeat.com
Select the menu to find various model sheets from cartoons for you to practise with. Why not have a go at copying some classic characters such as the Flintstones?

http://www.cartoonster.com
Online step-by-step tutorials to help you get started in animation.

http://www.geocities.com/nmaniatis/bricktastic/walktute.htm
A tutorial to help you make Lego characters appear to walk more convincingly in your Brickmation films.

http://www.karmatoons.com
The website of Doug Compton, a US cartoonist and animator. Includes games and helpful animation tutorials.

http://www.mocpages.com
A list of Brickmation films.

http://www.pdi.com/
DreamWorks Animation's website.

http://www.pixar.com/
The website of Pixar Animation Studios.

Disclaimer
All the Internet addresses (URLs) given in this book were valid at the time of going to press. However, owing to the dynamic nature of the Internet, some addresses may have changed or sites may have ceased to exist since publication. While the author, packager, and publishers regret any inconvenience this may cause readers, no responsibility for any such change can be accepted by the author, packager, or publishers.

Index

Titles in the *Art off the wall* series include:

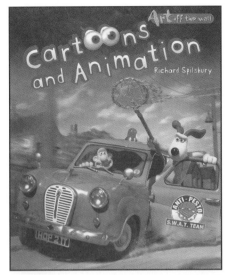

Hardback   978-0-431-01473-9

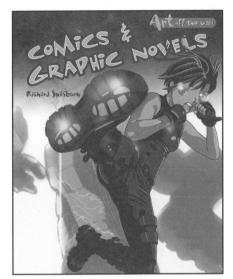

Hardback   978-0-431-01472-2

Hardback   978-0-431-01474-6

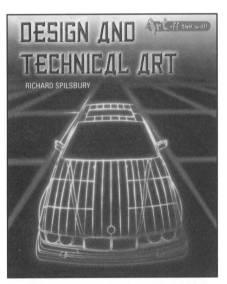

Hardback   978-0-431-01475-3

Hardback   978-0-431-01476-0

Find out about other titles from Heinemann Library on our website www.heinemann.co.uk/library